ENVIRONMENTS

Greg Roza

Rosen Classroom Books & Materials™
New York

Published in 2006 by The Rosen Publishing Group, Inc.
29 East 21st Street, New York, NY 10010

Book Design: Erica Clendening

Photo Credits: Cover, pp. 1, 7 (Tree, Mushrooms), 14 © Digital Vision; p. 4–5 © ROB & SAS/Corbis; p. 7 (Petri Dish & Hand) © Lester Lefkowitz/Corbis; p. 7 (Horse) © Digital Stock; p. 7 (Sky) © Weatherstock; p. 8 (Winter) © Eyewire; p. 8 (Desert) © Ron Watts/Corbis; p. 11 © Kennan Ward/Corbis; p. 12 © Tom Bean/Corbis

ISBN: 1-4042-5815-9
6-pack ISBN: 1-4042-5816-7

Manufactured in China

Contents

What Is an Environment?

Many kinds of environments can be found on Earth. An environment is made up of many living things as well as nonliving things, such as water, light, and soil. The living things and nonliving things that make up an environment are all part of a web of **relationships** that scientists call an **ecosystem**.

Your environment includes the people you live with, the animals and the plants that you see, and the foods you eat. It also includes nonliving things such as weather and water.

Living Things

A natural environment has plants, animals, and **microscopic** life-forms. Living things in an environment often depend on each other to survive. Some living things need other living things as a source of food. Some living things depend on others to keep them safe from their enemies. Removing one type of living thing from an environment can affect all the other living things in that environment.

Scientists know of more than 1.4 million types of living things on Earth.

Nonliving Things

In addition to living things, environments are filled with nonliving things. The nonliving things that help to define an environment include weather, **temperature**, soil, air, water, and sunlight.

Living things need nonliving things to survive. Together, the living things and nonliving things that make up an ecosystem create a balance of nature. Changing or removing just one of these things could upset the balance.

Temperature is the nonliving element that affects snow in the winter and heat in the summer.

What Is Adaptation?

Adaptation is a **trait** of living things that allows them to live in their natural environment. Sometimes a natural environment can change. If living things have adaptations for the new environment, they will survive. However, if the living things are not adapted, they may become **extinct**. Living things may also move to a new environment when the one they have lived in has changed.

The arctic fox has gray fur in the summer, but its fur turns white in the winter. This adaptation allows the arctic fox to hide easily in deep snow. The fox is able to hunt for food and stay safe from its enemies.

Biomes

Major types of environments around the world are called **biomes**. A land biome is defined by its **climate** and the plants and other living things that are found there. A biome that occurs in one area of the world can sometimes be found thousands of miles away in another area. The plants and the animals living in a biome have adapted to life there over many years. They have special traits that allow them to survive in their biome.

This is a picture of a grasslands biome in South Dakota, USA. Grasslands with tall grasses are called prairies.

Biomes Around the World

There are many types of biomes on Earth. Desert biomes receive less than ten inches of rain a year and have few plants because the soil is so dry. The tundra biomes are extremely cold areas where there are no trees. Rain forest biomes receive more than 100 inches of rain a year and contain the widest range of plants and animals found on Earth. Prairie biomes are flat grasslands that have very few trees.

Glossary

biomes Major natural environments.

climate The kind of weather a place has over a long period of time.

ecosystem A community of living and nonliving things, and the connections between them.

extinct No longer existing.

microscopic Something that cannot be seen without a microscope.

relationships Connections between two or more things.

temperature How hot or cold something is.

trait A certain quality.

Index